A NEW HOPE

FOR MICHAEL

MICHAEL DEON

PAGE PUBLISHING
Conneaut Lake, PA

First originally published by Page Publishing 2024

ISBN 979-8-88793-616-1 (pbk)
ISBN 979-8-88793-625-3 (digital)

Printed in the United States of America

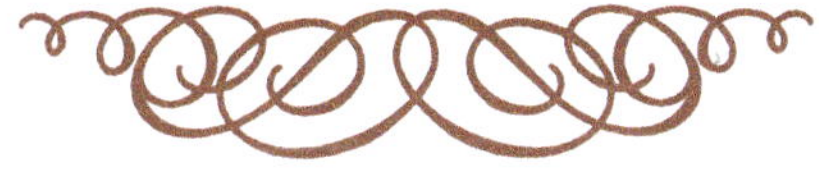

Our story began on a cold afternoon in Detroit. A football game at Cooley High School was about to end. Cooley High School Cardinals was playing against the Mumford High School Mustangs for the city championship. There was thirty seconds left on the game clock. Mumford had possession of the ball. Mumford chose to pass the ball. The ball was intercepted and ran in for a touchdown. The final score was twenty-one to fourteen Cooley. Two of the Cardinals, cousins Floyd and Michael, ran past the Mustang's bench, talking trash along the way.

Cooley High School Cardinals played against the Mumford Mustangs. The rivalry had been going on since the fifties, and Mumford had more wins, so it was intense.

2

"Y'all may have won last year, but this year, we gon' beat y'all. It's the men playing against the boys," Mumford said.

Cooley said, "Nah. It's the men playing against the girls."

"Oh, yeah, well, I hear y'all mama said y'all have a hard time finding dates," Mumford said.

"Oh, y'all calling us mama's boys. Okay, we gone see about that," said Cooley.

"Hey, Michael, I know where the party is going to be. We can go celebrate my ESPN highlight catch," Floyd said.

"Yeah, right. It wasn't even that magnificent. You almost fumbled it," Michael replied.

"That's okay. The next time you run a punt, return back. I am going to help our opponent tackle you," said Floyd.

"I don't think those college recruits from Michigan University would take that kindly to our coach," Michael replied. "You will end up sitting so far on the bench, I will have to call long distance to speak to you."

"Yeah, right," said Floyd.

"So what's up with this party you mentioned? And please tell me it's not over one of those metaphysical thinking friend of yours' house again," said Michael.

"Well, uh…" Floyd replied.

"I hope it's not at that house we used to pass when we were kids with the funny smell coming out of it like the dead is walking around inside there."

"After all these years, you shouldn't be nervous about the house anymore."

"Well, tell that to the cops. The cops don't even go in there."

"Well, a friend of mine told me that it is at that house. Let's just go by there and check it out."

"Man, Rick must be inventing his own holidays to celebrate," said Michael.

"Now, I know you have heard about his parties. There are plenty of beautiful women, and there are no drugs allowed in his crib."

"Selling that BS on the street," Michael said sarcastically. "He is a hypocrite drug dealer. If he had those same standards on the streets, it would reduce crime."

"Yeah. That's because he sold all of his supplies and there is not anymore left to pass out," replied Michael. "Well, he read that book 'Being a Drug Dealer for Dummies.'"

"Alright. That did it! You dissin' me and my boy. My honor needs to be restored. It's time for a duel," said Floyd.

"Dang! You always call me out when I have the wrong shoes on," replied Michael.

"That's right. And you know the drill. I determine how long and the path of the race," said Floyd. "See that brown house the one with the satellite dish on top of the roof? That's our finish line," Floyd continued.

"Alright. I got cha," said Michael.

"And, oh yes, obstacles," said Floyd.

"Obstacles!" Shouted Michael.

"When one player yells 'Obstacles!', you do whatever you can to get around or through them. This is a no-excuse race. Alright. At the sound of this quarter hitting the ground, the race will begin," Floyd said.

"Haha. You have lost already. You are about to lose your money. You are—" replied Michael.

"Whipping your behind in this race will make you forget about this quarter," Floyd said.

Floyd tossed the quarter in the air. The quarter made a distinctive sound as it landed on the pavement. *Ting!* Floyd and Michael were off in a flash. After dodging some people and cars and outrunning a bus, Floyd and Michael arrived at their destination of Floyd's friend's house. They ran through an alley to reach it. Upon reaching the house, they had to jump the backyard fence. After clearing the backyard fence, they noticed a surprise waiting for them. There were two furious, breath-stinking Rottweiler dogs noticing them. Floyd and Michael both let out splitting yells. They both started running like they were one hundred-yard Olympic dashers toward the next fence. One of the dogs almost caught Floyd. Then, suddenly, within a tenth of a second, the dog had a chain attached to him, and someone they cannot see was holding it. When one of the dogs almost caught Floyd, he said with a terrified look on his face, "What the—"

Then immediately the angel grabbed the chain. Then, just as suddenly, the being disappeared.

"Whew, that was close!" Floyd said while catching his breath.

"Yes, I saw your life flash right before my eyes."

"Wait a minute. Don't you mean you saw your life flash right before your eyes? asked Floyd.

"No, I didn't stutter. I mean I saw your life flash before my eyes. My life has been too uneventful for any flashbacks, even for me," Michael answered.

"Uh-huh. That's a bunch of crap, and you know it. Besides, I won," said Floyd.

"Yeah, right. It was like a tie, and I gave you a head start," replied Michael.

Floyd turned and looked toward the house they were standing in front of.

"Hey, isn't this your friend's house? asked Michael.

"It sure is," answered Floyd.

The house had windows that were boarded up, and the windows that were not were mirror windows that caused you to see your reflection and not inside. Weeds had outgrown. There was chipped paint, and the awning was hanging sideways. The backyard smelled like dogs.

"I am not going in there. This looks like the house of Ma, Pa, cockroaches, and their cousins, the rats," said Michael.

"Trust me," said Floyd.

When Floyd said "Trust me," Michael raised his eyebrow and said, "Yeah, right. Now you have done gone and done it. Every time you say that, somehow, some way means trouble."

Michael and Floyd walked up the stairs and then on to the porch.

"Yeah, right. And besides like I said, he doesn't allow any drugs or smoking in his house," stated Floyd.

"Ain't that ironic?" Michael asked. "A drug dealer saying 'no' to drugs in his crib. He ain't saying that while his boys are out there selling that BS on the street."

Floyd knocked on the door. A beautiful woman dressed in red opened the door.

"Well, now, if it isn't the heroes. Let me see some ID," she said.

Michael said, "What do you need IDs for? We are all underage."

She said, "Yeah, but y'all look like y'all still in junior high school. I need y'all high school IDs."

Floyd said, "Show me yours, and I'll show you mine."

She said, "Well, if you were this quick on the football field, you would be undefeated."

Floyd said, Oh, well, we can use some more cheerleaders."

Michael said, "Are you going to let us in or what?"

She said, "Keep it up, and y'all might have to use the back entrance."

She rolled her eyes and reluctantly let them in.

Michael said, "You know what, man, after that exchange, beauty is only skin-deep."

Then Floyd said, "I think she might like me."

Michael said, "She acts like she goes for guys much older."

Floyd replied, "Well, she did wink at me."

Michael said, "Well, she probably had something in her eye."

Floyd said, "Aw, man, you just jealous that she winked at me, and not you."

Michael said, "Yeah, right. Well, I'm going to allow you to have your fantasy."

"That's my boy's girlfriend, so stop drooling!" Floyd said. "You was just trying to get with her."

Michael said, "I'm not drooling. But if your boy was a mind reader, he would be pissed with me right now."

Then Floyd and Michael started moving toward the party.

"Hey, Rick, what's up?" asked Floyd.

"My bank account, if that's any of your business," Rick answered.

"Yeah, man," Floyd said. "Hey, this is my cousin Michael."

"I supposed he's been briefed," said Floyd.

Michael said with his head down, "No smoking. No drinking. No looking Rick in the eye."

"Oh, really?" Rick replied. "Take y'all briefed behind downstairs, and have some fun."

Michael and Floyd walked down a flight of stairs.

"Is he always flat like that, with grit teeth?"

Floyd said, "Yeah. Because of the game he is involved in, he always has to keep up his guard. But after you get to know him, you just get used to it. But he's cool."

As they reached the bottom of the stairs, they beheld a lavishly furnished living room with plenty of floor space for mingling and dancing. The living room was filled with students who were celebrating the Cardinals' victory over the Mustangs for the championship. The party music was loud, but not overbearing.

The living room had flashing party lights with two tan leather couches. It was clean. The DJ was playing the song, "Disco Inferno."

"Wow, talk about what's important on the inside," said Michael.

"I told you it would be alright," Floyd said grinning.

Floyd and Michael did not stay in shock of their surroundings for long.

Floyd said, "Well, it's time to throw down and have some fun. Let's pick up one of these girls and start dancing! That's my jam!"

"Oh, that girl looks like she can dance." They noticed two girls talking on the other side of the room. They walked up to them.

Michael said, "Would y'all like to dance?"

The ladies nodded yes.

Floyd started doing the robot dance wrong in a jerking motion. Michael said, "What you doing, man? You got to go to the bathroom?"

Floyd's dance partner said, "I was wondering the same thing."

Then the DJ announced, "Hey, y'all, let's get ready for a game. We need two brave guys to take part in the smell game. How about y'all two, especially the one with the herky-jerky move?"

Michael said, "See that, man? Now you putting us on the spot. Now we have to go ahead and do this."

While Floyd and Michael were enjoying the festivities, they did not notice that two disturbed students were glaring at them from the opposite side of the floor.

The two upset guys from the game was over the smell test.

"Every time they win, they always talk trash. You got that stuff on you, man?" said one of them.

"Yeah, I got it," said the other.

"Then give it to me. We gone set these guys straight because they talk too much trash."

"Yeah, okay. We're going to see who will get the last laugh," the other replied.

Soon afterward, one of them turned off the music and told everyone it's time to play the smell game and that the first prize is one hundred dollars.

"Smell game?" Michael asked. "What in the heck is that?"

"Well, it's like we blindfold a player, and they have to identify what is in front of them by smelling it and guessing what it is. And whoever guesses the most correctly wins the loot," said the other thug.

"And what are we smelling?" Floyd asked.

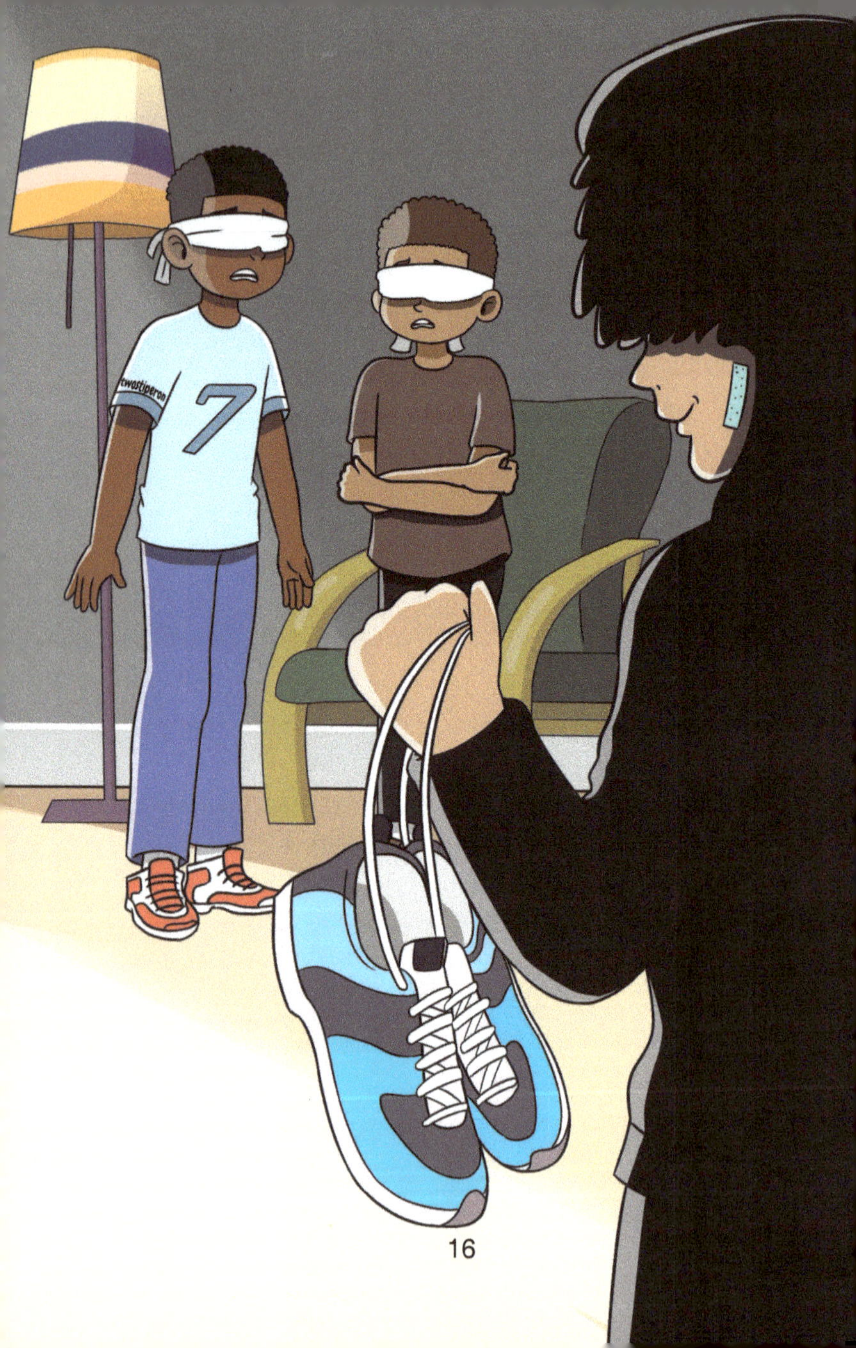
twostiperoo
7
16

"Whatever we get to choose," said the guy. "The purpose of the game is for you to guess what it is, anyway. And since you were the last to get here, why don't you go first?"

Floyd and Michael had their reservations about this so-called smell game, especially by it being explained by this degenerate. But for the sake of not being rude, they accepted the challenge.

"Don't worry. It will be fun. No one is going to do anything stupid," said the guy.

Floyd and Michael were seated in the two front chairs, blindfolded, in the middle of the living room. The game started off innocent enough. Floyd and Michael sniffed some rice pudding, cottage cheese, hamburger, and sardines. But the two juvenile delinquents from Mumford had other ideas. Both guys took a shoe off and laced it with cocaine they had snuck in the party.

"All right, you two," one said, "guess this one, and you both will win one hundred dollars on us."

"Come on with it!" challenged Floyd.

With that said, Floyd and Michael took a deep sniff. Cocaine came out of the shoes and into their nostrils. Floyd and Michael both fell out of their chairs and on the floor. Floyd tried to get up, but he was physically not able. The poison was doing its job.

"What the—!" screamed Rick. "You dare bring that stuff in my crib! You two idiots are out of here!" Rick motioned to his boys, signaling them to put those idiots out of his house. Rick and his cronies did attack two guys. But the two football players did not leave easily. During the melee, Floyd and Michael were mentally out of it. They didn't realize that there was an actual fight going on around them. They acted as if they were being entertained by a movie, for common sense had been interrupted. Two of the young ladies out of the crowd grabbed Michael and Floyd and led them through the side exit. The ladies wiped their faces off with cold towels along the way.

"What's wrong with me?" Floyd asked while wiping his nose. "What is this?"

"Man, we've been—" Michael tried to gather his thoughts together, but he could not at the moment. The young ladies were able to guide them home, for they knew the way to go. They were angels sent from heaven. As time passed, that experience did have a negative effect on their lives. They both would have cravings for that sensation from the first hit again. It was a sensation they could not fulfill, a glass of water they could not fill.

Months later, Michael and his family returned from church one Sunday morning. His family consisted of his mother, Irene, whose very being was the one that helped hold the church together. His sister, Denise, a very smart honor roll student, unfortunately had a bad temper. Last but not the least, his father was the Reverend Odell P. Price. Reverend Price's fiery sermons set preaching to a higher standard. Reverend Price's messages were filled with truthfulness and wisdom. The Reverend was a very passionate man with his own set of rules. This behavior could sometimes be overbearing and unnerving. The love ran deep in the Price family, even through daring times of family confrontations. Oh yeah, can't forget Michael's grandmother, Annie Mae Price. Michael's grandmother was the family matriarch and spiritual leader. Annie Mae also had the gift of reciting chapters from the Bible from memory.

"Denise, I thought you were going to teach Sunday school every Sunday morning," said Reverend Odell.

"Oh, Daddy, I know I told you that I was going to make that commitment," Denise replied, "but I have to go at my own pace."

"Well, I need you to be there next Sunday," said Reverend Odell. "Otherwise, you would be setting a bad example for the other leaders in the church."

"Dad, what did I tell you?" Denise replied, "Most of the time, you are late getting to church yourself."

"Now look," Reverend Odell said, "you just do as I suggested."

"You mean as you just *ordered*, don't you?" Denise said in a smart manner.

"I'll tell you what," Reverend Odell said, "you better watch your mouth before I—" Reverend Odell did not get a chance to finish his sentence before Denise immediately pulled out a ten-inch butcher knife.

"Look, you are never going to lay your hands on me again!" Denise cried.

Michael screamed in shock, "What in the world are you doing with that knife!"

Then Irene said, "Oh my God! Why would you feel the need to bring a knife?"

"Y'all can act blind and stupid if you want to, but y'all know what's going on between me and Daddy!"

Reverend Price said, "What do you mean? You are acting like a fool."

Denise replied, "Well I don't have to hear this." She attempted to jump out of the van while it was moving, but the doors locked unexpectedly. If she would have jumped at that moment, she would have leaped into oncoming traffic, and she would have perished.

Denise said in frustration, "This raggedy old van. It figures that the door won't open when you want it to."

She did not know that a miracle just happened.

Michael said, "It's still no reason to pull out a knife."

Denise said, "The last time Daddy whipped me was because I misplaced his glue. I am fifteen years old. I am too old to be getting whippings, especially over something stupid. You know how Daddy treats us. He is always the preacher and never just our father."

Reverend Price started to interrupt by saying, "Well—"

Then Irene intervened and said, "Don't interrupt. Just listen."

Then Reverend Odell said, "Let me pull over so I can listen."

Denise said, "Finally, you're listening! Daddy, a preacher doesn't take the stress out on his children. You so concerned with the church growing that you don't mind our family breaking apart. We only go out to eat when the church goes out to eat. We only travel when the church is having a convention. We only talk when it's church business."

Michael said, "Well, Dad. Sometimes, we do need you to relax and have family time and not always be this stern preacher. Church is great, but we need just plain old family time too."

Denise said, "We growing up before your eyes, and you still whopping us like we li'l kids."

Reverend Odell said, "Y'all know what I am trying to do for the Lord. Aren't y'all overreacting just a little bit?"

Annie Mae said the scripture, "Fathers, provoke not your children to wrath. Children, honor your mother and father, and also Odell, the children are right. We should put God first, but also we should not exclude good, old-fashioned family time.

Irene said, "Odell, no matter how much the church grows, God still gave us these children."

Reverend Odell said, "Maybe I have been over-occupied with having the church to grow, and I have been feeling a lot of stress."

Denise said with tears in her eyes, "Dad, just do the best you can, and let God take care of the rest."

Then Annie Mae said calmly, "Amen."

The doors would unlock themselves moments later, for they were close to their home. The family did reach their home safely. They talked things out, and calmness did prevail.

Night had fallen, and Floyd and Michael were out walking. These two young men were feeling quite desperate, and they were hungry. They were not hungry for what a Thanksgiving feast could satisfy. They were hungry for a false hope. They yearned for a chemical reaction that sends a dangerous, raging storm into their inner universe. Most people associate darkness with danger or evilness. On that night, these two young men needed the light.

"Man, I am itching for another hit!" said Floyd.

"Well, if you are itching that hard, then you might as well go home and take a bath because there is no more loot in the chute," replied Michael.

"Yeah, well, there is some loot in my dad's house, and I know where he keeps his small change," said Floyd.

"Wait a minute. How small is the change you are talking about?" Michael asked. "About ten or twenty cents?"

"Naw, man! Ten or maybe twenty dollars," Floyd answered.

"Oh, great. That makes me feel really eager to help you steal from your own father," Michael said sarcastically.

"Hey, come on. Let's go. He's not going to miss it. Look, his car is not here, and the house is dark," said Floyd. "I know a window on the side of the house where the lock doesn't work very well."

They both went on the side of the house and found the window that Floyd spoke of. Floyd then climbed on top of Michael's shoulders so he can easily try to get the window open. Normally, since the two young men noticed that the house was dark, they assumed there would be no one home. Little did they know Floyd's father was home. His car was gone because it was in the repair shop.

"Hey, man, stop shaking. I almost—" Before Floyd could finish his sentence, a loud bang filled the air. Michael was familiar with this sound. However, he had always heard it down street or on someone else's block. This time, the sound was so close, it made his eardrums ring with pain. The sound was gunfire, gunfire that set a bullet into Floyd's chest, blowing him off Michael's shoulders as he somersaulted into the air. Though the somersault seemed to be instantaneous, for Floyd, it seemed to go by slowly. It seemed as if time stood still as Floyd had witnessed the things he had done in his life, whether it was good or bad. Before Floyd's body hit the ground, death had claimed its latest victim. Michael turned to take one look at Floyd and then ran because of fear. For the image of his cousin being shot was branded into his head. Michael felt fear and remorse that night that he had no idea where his feet was guiding. His subconscious mind was taking care of that. In the back of his head, he could hear a father's scream when he would finally realize what he had done. He had extinguished a flame that his seed helped him to create. Michael ran until it felt like his lungs were going to ignite. Finally, he saw a place where he could get some rest for his mind and his body. He found a place where he could find solace and comfort for his grief. Michael was relieved to see a church. As Michael entered the church, he could hear singing. The youth choir was rehearsing that night. The choir was singing a song of repentance and assurance. The choir sang about that righteous man who had fallen many times but got back up again and again. Michael ran downstairs in the church and into a room, slamming the

NOOOOOOO!

door behind him. The impact of the door knocked over a lit candle in the arts and crafts room that someone had neglected to put out. The small room right next to the one Michael was in soon became engulfed with flames.

"Oh, Lord, forgive me." Michael cried with tears streaming down his face. "I should have stopped him!" As Michael cried against the door, he could hear agonizing screams coming from upstairs. The screams awakened Michael's senses, and he then began to smell smoke as well.

"Oh, no! The church is on fire!" Michael screamed.

Michael grabbed the fire extinguisher off of the hallway wall as he ran toward the stairway. He courageously battled the fire all the way up the stairs until he approached the choir room where the kids were rehearsing. When Michael searched the choir room, he discovered that the smoke overwhelmed some of the children and the choir director. Michael saved the kids who were conscious by helping them escape through

a side window. Michael could have saved himself, but instead, he went back to see if he could save some more choir members. The gaseous smoke filled Michael's lungs, causing him to drift into unconsciousness. As he drifted into unconsciousness, he fell, he could only hear the wailing sounds of fire engines and emergency vehicles.

The firemen arrived and frantically entered into the raging inferno. The firemen rushed to each child, for it was a race against time, a race they would lose, for each time they brought a child out, it was lifeless. The fireman carried Michael's lifeless body out of the church. Michael's clock had stopped for his inner light could no longer be seen. Death was very busy that night. The firemen didn't want to lose hope, so they attempted to resuscitate some of the victims. Tears began to swell into some of the firemen's eyes as they desperately tried to hold their emotions in. By this time, residents from the church's neighborhood had arrived on the scene. The ambulance had arrived on the scene. The rescue teams loaded the children, as well as Michael's empty shell, into an ambulance. As the ambulance whirled off onto the night, some bystanders cried, and others were too shocked to release any emotion. Michael's family arrived to see who they could console in this time of sorrow. The family had no idea they would be the ones who would soon need the comforting. Some of the bystanders recognized Michael's family and informed them of Michael's act of bravery and sacrifice.

The paramedics' rescue attempt was in vain. Every one of the fire victims was pronounced to be DOA. Michael's family arrived at the hospital in just minutes after the ambulance did. Upon their arrival, Michael's family were notified about the dreadful news of the death of the children and their beloved Michael.

The bodies were moved to the hospital morgue downstairs while the investigation continued. Michael's family gathered themselves in the waiting room. Tears flowed freely as they felt shock and dismay.

Michael's sister, Denise, could not bear the pain.

"Why? Oh, why?" Denise asked. "Why would the Lord let this happen?"

"There was a time when I had to ask those questions," the Reverend said, choking back his tears. "There are times when we have to trust God through the good times and most definitely through the bad times, for the enemy would love for us to keep doubts in our hearts. We just have to trust God's love. For his love is so great, it cannot be measured. I know there are circumstances we do not understand but—"

"But what, Dad?" cried Denise. "I feel so hurt, sometimes I wish I could—"

"You could what, child?" Grandma interrupted.

"I don't know, Grandma," Denise answered. "Michael was doing the right thing. I mean, he saved those other kids' lives. Why is it that when he was doing right, he still got punished as if he was doing something wrong?"

"Denise, and we know that all things work together for good to them that love God, to them who are the called according to his purpose," replied Grandma (Romans 8:28 KJV). "One day, all of the things that leave us bewildered we will all understand. We have to have hope and trust in the Lord like the Reverend said. The Lord knows our burdens are heavy right now."

"Yes, Grandma. We have to have hope. But what we need right now is a new hope for Michael," said Denise.

"Let us all come together and seek the Lord," said Grandma.

With that said, everyone in the waiting room stopped what they were doing. Believers of Christ and unbelievers of Christ all joined hands and bowed down their heads as Grandma began to lead them in prayer. Grandma had been blessed with a spiritual gift of remembering whole chapters from the books of the Holy Bible.

"Michael, since you are not able to speak for yourself, we will speak for you." Grandma whispered as she started to pray.

"Oh, Lord, rebuke me not in thine anger, neither chasten me in thy hot displeasure. Have mercy upon me, oh, Lord. For I am weak. Oh, Lord, heal me. For my bones are vexed. My soul is also sore vexed. But thou, oh, Lord, how long? Return, oh, Lord, deliver my soul. Oh, save me for thy mercies' sake. For in death, there is no remembrance of thee. In the grave, who shall give thee thanks? I am weary with my groaning. All the night I make my bed to swim. I water my couch with my tears. Mine eyes are consumed because of grief. It waxeth old because of all my enemies. Depart from me all ye workers of iniquity, for the Lord hath heard a voice of my weeping. The Lord hath heard my supplications. The Lord will receive my prayer. Let all my enemies be ashamed and sore vexed. Let them return and be ashamed suddenly. Be merciful unto me, oh, God, be merciful unto me. For my soul trusteth in thee. Yea, in the shadow of thy wings, I will make my refuge, until these calamities be overpast. I will cry God Most High. Unto God that performeth all things for me. He shall send from heaven and save me from the reproach of him that would swallow me up. God send forth His mercy and His Truth. My soul is among lions, and I lie even among them that are set on fire. Even the sons of men whose teeth are spears and arrows and thy teeth a sharp sword. Be thou exalted, oh, God, above all heavens. Let thy glory be above all the earth. In Jesus's holy name. Amen."

As Grandma concluded the prayer, the family continued to hold hands and repeated "Yes, Lord!" among themselves.

Meanwhile, there was a disagreement downstairs in the morgue.

"Turn that radio down!" says one of the morgue's attendants.

"Why?" said the other attendant. "I mean, they are all asleep. It's not like they are going to wake up."

"Have some respect for the dead. This could be one of your relatives in those freezers," said the nurse filling out some paperwork.

"Oh, that would be just fine," the attendant answered. "I come from a family that has a passion for music. Except they do like all that no-brain gangster rap. I can't stand that—"

"Wait, did you hear that?" interrupted the other morgue attendant as he turned down the radio so he could listen more carefully.

"*Thump! Thump! Thump!*" Went the noise.

"Hey! I heard that," the nurse said. "Where is that coming from?"

They began to look all around the morgue, rejecting the obvious answer.

"*Thump! Thump! Thump!*" The noise went again. They suddenly stood still and stared at each other, realizing the impossible.

"*Eeeeeek!*" The nurse screamed, pointing toward the freezer. "It's coming from one of those chutes." The nurse screamed so loud, the hospital security guards and Michael's family upstairs heard

AHHHH!
THUMP!
THUMP!

her. They all ran downstairs to investigate. The guards came into the morgue first.

"What's the problem?" asked one of them.

"*Thump! Thump! Thump!*" went the noise again.

"Does that answer your question?" said one of the morgue attendants.

One of the guards walked over to a noisy chute to pull it open. All of a sudden, the body that lay in the chute began to sit up. Screams filled the room, causing some of the witnesses to run away. The guards pulled their guns out. The sheet that was covering the body fell so that they could see the person underneath it.

Michael sat up and said, "Hi, Grandma!"

"Hallelujah! Oh, Lord, your wonders are great," cried Grandma.

"Thank you, Jesus! Thank you." The family shouted as tears flowed freely again. This time, happy tears were being shed. Out of curiosity, the guard began to check the other chutes, and they found the children who had died in the fire alive again.

Miraculously, all of the victims were alive again. In the midst of it all, the two cousins were reunited. Floyd was alive again. The evil that once tormented them tormented them no more.

Out of nowhere, angels appeared among the rejoicing crowd.

"Oh, death, where is thy sting? Oh, grave, where is thy victory?" Grandma shouted. "God's love endureth forever and ever!"

Death appeared and walked toward Grandma. The angels protected her by blocking death's intended target. Death departed as quickly as it came.

"Amen, Grandma. Amen." Denise cried.

Pray because God listens.

The End

ABOUT THE AUTHOR

Michael Deon is passionate about the Word of God. He has been a believer in Christ since he can remember. He loves to discuss and post positive spiritual messages on social media and loves to participate in gospel plays. He also loves to sing gospel music on YouTube. His favorite team is his home team, the Detroit Lions, because he has hope. He spreads messages about having hope in God.

9 798888 793616 1